t-04

$\frac{X}{\cdot/10}$

✓ CR

West Point

CORNERSTONES OF FREEDOM™

SECOND SERIES

Heidi Kimmel

Children's Press®
A Division of Scholastic Inc.
New York • Toronto • London • Auckland • Sydney
Mexico City • New Delhi • Hong Kong
Danbury, Connecticut

Photographs © 2004: AP/Wide World Photos/Jim Mcknight: cover top;
Corbis Images: 11, 20, 26, 36, 38, 45 right (Bettmann), 23 (Hulton-
Deutsch Collection), cover bottom, 25 bottom, 30, 31, 32, 33 (Bob Krist),
27 (Robert Maass), 14, 24 (Lee Snider), 37 (Joseph Sohm/ChromoSohm
Inc.), 7, 22; David J. Forbert: 3, 4, 45 left; Folio, Inc.: 39 (Phoebe Bell), 6
(Jon Riley); Hulton|Archive/Getty Images: 13; Library of Congress: 8, 18;
Magnum Photos: 29 (Susan Meiselas), 21 (Wayne Miller); North Wind
Picture Archives: 19; Photri Inc.: 28, 45 center (Mark E. Gibson), 35
(Nick Sebastian), 10, 15 bottom, 16, 17, 19 top, 44 top left, 44 center;
Stock Montage, Inc.: 25 top, 44 top right (The Newberry Library), 12;
The Image Works/Photri/Topham: 40; West Point Museum Art
Collection, United States Military Academy: 9.

Library of Congress Cataloging-in-Publication Data
Kimmel, Heidi.
West Point / Heidi Kimmel.
p. cm. — (Cornerstones of freedom. Second series)
Summary: Chronicles the history of the military academy at West Point,
New York, including its role in the American Revolution, the Mexican
War, the Civil War, and World Wars I and II, and discusses the daily life
of a cadet and the enrollment of minorities.
Includes bibliographical references and index.
ISBN 0-516-24230-X
1. United States Military Academy—Juvenile literature. [1. United
States Military Academy—History.] I. Title. II. Series.
U410.L1K55 2003
355'.0071'173—dc21

2003009099

I T IS R-DAY, THE DAY NEW CADETS report to West Point for six weeks of Cadet Basic Training, also known as Beast Barracks. The new cadets are lined up outside Michie Stadium, bags in hand. Many of them have heard about the difficulties of this day from older family members or other people. The cadets, along with their families, are allowed to enter in groups of one hundred. They take seats low in the stadium, close to the field. After hearing several speeches, a firstie, or senior, addresses the incoming class: "At this time, I'd like to ask the candidates to move down the steps with your baggage ... You have ninety seconds to say your goodbyes."

Parents, brothers, and sisters gather on the lawn at West Point to share important events, such as R-Day and graduation, with the cadets.

* * * *

By the time the cadets get another glimpse of their families that afternoon, they will have been issued large blue bags full of supplies and clothing. They will have been fitted for their dress uniforms, given haircuts, and sent to drill stations to learn to march. They will have learned the only four responses they are allowed: "Yes, sir (or ma'am)," "No, sir," "No excuse, sir," and "Sir, I do not understand." But most important, they will have tried their hardest to obey the orders that were shouted at them for countless hours, and they are now closer to being soldiers than to being the young high school graduates who presented themselves a few hours ago.

Later that afternoon, parents gather on the Plain, a flat patch of grass in front of the **barracks**, and watch their children, now dressed in summer uniforms, march out to take their oaths. "I do solemnly swear that I will support the Constitution of the United States, and bear true allegiance to the National Government, that I will maintain and defend the **sovereignty** of the United States . . . and that I will at all times obey the orders of my superior officers, and the Uniform Code of the United States." The cadet companies, or groups, pass in review (a formal inspection), marching at precisely 120 steps per minute. Family members strain their eyes to pick out their loved ones. Then the cadets disappear into the buildings from which they came.

WEST POINT: ITS HISTORY

After flowing south with hardly a twist or turn for 200 miles (320 kilometers), the Hudson River runs directly into a

★ ★ ★ ★

The location of West Point on the Hudson River has been called "the key to the country" for its strategic importance.

flat-topped **promontory** that forces it to make a sharp turn to the east. Once past this barrier, the river turns back to its original southward course, forming an *S*-shaped curve, and continues south to New York City and the Atlantic Ocean. The spot at which the river turns sharply is known not only for being one of the most beautiful places in the country but also for being the location of West Point.

Many of the leaders who have shaped United States history from the Revolutionary War to this day once stood at this site. General George Washington, commander in chief

This illustration shows a view of West Point and the area surrounding it in its early days.

of the Continental army, recognized West Point's geographic importance in defending the colonies against the superior British forces. He called it "the key to the country." It is also remembered as the scene of another brilliant U.S. general's act of **treason** (see p.10).

West Point is best known, however, for the military academy that our founding fathers established there. In every war the United States has been involved in, the leaders of our country's land forces attended the United States Military Academy at West Point. Graduates of West Point have also made their mark on U.S. history in other ways, some building the railroads and canals that opened up the vast resources of the United States, some surveying the dangerous, unexplored territories of the West. Two of West Point's graduates would be elected president of the United States, and two would walk on the moon. Today, male and female cadets at the military academy come from all over the United States and from every economic and ethnic background. They all share the experience of learning to lead while drilling on the Plain at this legendary place on the Hudson River.

The importance of West Point's location became clear during the Revolutionary War. The British had captured New York City and were pursuing General Washington's

Fort Putnam, built in 1778, was one of many forts at West Point during the American Revolution.

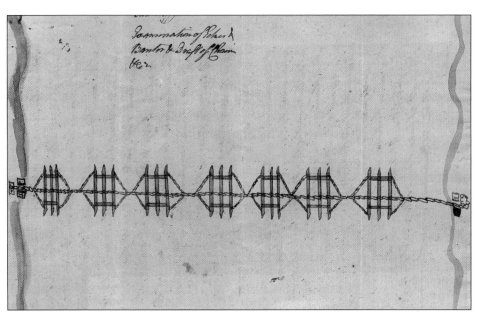

This historic drawing of the Great Chain, which blocked the Hudson River at West Point, dates back to January 1777.

troops north. If the British could gain control of the Hudson River, they could cut off New England from the rest of the colonies. The British had already destroyed the first crude forts that were built in the area, so in 1777 Washington ordered the commander of the Continental forces in that region to "employ your whole force and all the means in your power for erecting and completing . . . such works and obstructions as may be necessary to defend and secure the river against any future attempts of the enemy."

To make sure no British ships could travel up the Hudson River, it was decided that a great iron chain should be stretched across the river at its narrowest point, from West Point to Constitution Island. When the chain was finished in 1778, it weighed 150 tons (136 metric tons). Each link weighed about 100 pounds (45 kilograms) and was 1,700 feet (518 meters) long. To stretch the chain across the river,

TRAITOR IN THE RANKS

Benedict Arnold was one of the great heroes of the American Revolution before he became a **traitor**. It wasn't until Arnold was appointed commander of West Point that he turned against America. He offered to deliver West Point to the British for 20,000 pounds and a brigadier general's commission in the British army. His plan was discovered, however, and Arnold managed to escape to the British ship *Vulture*, which was anchored in the Hudson River.

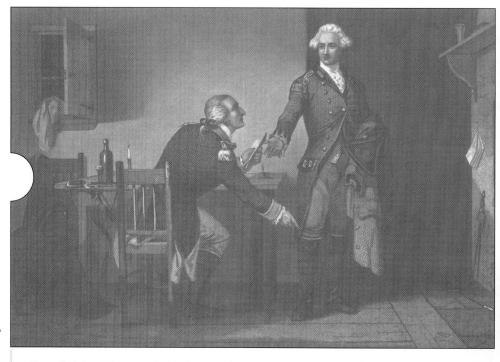

Benedict Arnold persuaded John André, a British major, to hide the plans for West Point in his boot. André was stopped and searched by American militiamen, who discovered the hidden papers.

it had to be placed on logs and floated across. Its ends were secured to capstones on each shore. Today, thirteen links are on display at West Point; the rest were sold as scrap metal after the war. The British never breached, or broke through, this chain.

THE BEGINNINGS OF THE MILITARY ACADEMY

As early as 1783, George Washington had proposed that West Point be turned into a military academy in which to train future officers. Between 1784 and 1794, a single company of soldiers occupied West Point. Its job was to maintain the crumbling fort. A corps, or military unit, of **artillerymen** and **engineers** was created and stationed at West Point in 1794.

Thomas Jefferson, Washington's secretary of state, was against the creation of a military academy. He opposed having an army of full-time soldiers because he did not want to create a permanent military class. In Europe, having "standing armies" led to rebellions because their officers

Buildings made of heavy logs, called blockhouses, helped protect the area of West Point.

* ⋆ ⋆ ⋆

were part of the upper class. They were often used to keep rulers in power and deprive citizens of their civil liberties. In spite of Jefferson's opposition, however, Washington never forgot the place where he had spent so much of the Revolution. Two days before his death in 1799, Washington wrote to Alexander Hamilton, then inspector general of the army, still pushing for the establishment of a military academy at West Point.

When Thomas Jefferson became president in 1801, the young nation faced the problem of pirates attacking its ships and threats of foreign interference as a result of European control of the Louisiana Territory and Canada. In addition, the new country was in need of engineers to build bridges, roads, and canals during peacetime. (In Europe, military academies trained soldiers to be engineers.)

To address these needs, in March 1802 President Jefferson signed an act of Congress to establish the United States Military Academy, also known as West Point. The first class was made up of only ten cadets. They lived in the Revolutionary War barracks, ate their meals in neighboring houses, and went to class whenever they felt like attending. Their ages ranged from twelve to thirty years.

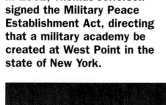

In 1802, Thomas Jefferson signed the Military Peace Establishment Act, directing that a military academy be created at West Point in the state of New York.

SYLVANUS THAYER, FATHER OF THE MILITARY ACADEMY

Sylvanus Thayer, a twenty-one-year-old Dartmouth College graduate, entered West Point when it was only five years old. Following his graduation, he taught mathematics at the academy until he left to fight in the War of 1812. After observing first-hand U.S. defeats caused by poor **scouting**, lack of knowledge of warfare, and jealousy among the officers, he decided to dedicate his life to the improvement of the U.S. Army. The U.S. government sent him to France in 1815 to study its military schools and to buy books and scientific equipment for the academy.

In 1817 President James Monroe appointed Brevet Major Sylvanus Thayer to be the U.S. Military Academy's fifth superintendent, or officer in charge of running the school. Thayer earned the title "Father of the Military Academy" by successfully guiding West Point through its early years. Thayer established the academy as a four-year institution of higher learning, with studies consisting of engineering, science, and the military arts. He developed the moral and ethical character (knowing right from wrong

Sylvanus Thayer served as superintendent of West Point from 1817 to 1833.

The Thayer Monument was erected on the West Point campus in 1883.

and conducting one's self accordingly) of the students, insisting on strict discipline and high principles. Classes contained only twelve to fifteen students, and each student was sent to the blackboard and graded every day. Each day, Thayer was presented with a written report about each student.

Under his guidance, West Point became recognized as the best engineering school in the country. In the years following the Civil War, West Point became the country's leading supplier of civil engineers, who constructed most of the young nation's first railway lines, roads, bridges, and harbors. Thayer resigned in 1833, after laying the foundation of West Point's structure and creating its code of conduct.

WEST POINT AND THE CIVIL WAR

As the 1860s approached, talk of war was everywhere, including West Point. Cadets argued about whether a state had the right to withdraw from the United States. There were many reasons for the conflict between North and South, but the most significant problems arose from differences in their way of life. Having an

14

agriculture-based economy, the Southern states depended on slave labor to plant and pick their crops. The Northern states had a manufacturing economy, where paid workers created a variety of goods in factories. Southerners believed that if Abraham Lincoln were elected president, he would try to abolish, or end, slavery in the United States.

Lincoln was elected president in November 1860, but did not take office until March 1861. In December 1860 South Carolina seceded, or withdrew, from the United States. Six more Southern states soon followed. The states that seceded set up a government that selected Jefferson Davis, member of West Point's class of 1828, to be president. These states became known as the Confederacy. The

Jefferson Davis (center left), a West Point graduate, was elected president of the Confederacy.

Brigadier General Beauregard graduated from West Point in 1838. He directed Confederate forces in the bombardment of Fort Sumter, the event that touched off the Civil War.

states that remained loyal to the United States came to be called the Union.

On April 12, 1861, Confederate forces ordered U.S. troops to leave Fort Sumter in South Carolina's Charleston Harbor. President Lincoln refused. This greatly angered the rest of the slave states, as they were called; eventually four more Southern states seceded. Before U.S. forces arrived, Confederate troops under the command of Pierre G. T. Beauregard fired on the fort. These were the first shots of the Civil War, and the fort was quickly surrendered to Confederate forces.

When West Point cadets from the Northern states heard about the attack, they gathered in the room of Cadet Harris of New York. They sang "The Star-Spangled Banner" so loudly that it was said the national anthem could be heard all the way across the Hudson River. With heavy hearts at having to give up their friends and the careers for which they had worked so hard, Southern cadets began to resign from the academy, refusing to take sides against their families and their home states. Of the eighty-six cadets from the South, sixty-five resigned. Choosing sides was a difficult decision not only for the cadets but also for the alumni, or graduates, of West

A group of West Point cadets posed for this photograph in 1863.

Point. There were 977 graduates who were still alive when the war began. Of those, 259 joined the Confederate forces (including 32 Northerners) and 638 fought for the Union forces (including 39 Southerners).

ROBERT E. LEE

Robert E. Lee (right) graduated second in his class from the U.S. Military Academy in 1829. In 1852 he was appointed superintendent of West Point and served until 1855. Lee was recognized as one of the best officers in the U.S. Army and was offered command of the Northern forces. A native Virginian, he decided to reject the offer because he did not want to fight against his home state. He regretfully resigned from the U.S. Army after thirty-two years of distinguished service, even though he was against secession.

Having gained valuable military experience during the Mexican and Indian wars, West Point graduates filled the highest ranks on both sides of the fighting during the Civil War. With 151 Confederate and about 294 Union generals who were graduates of West Point, the Civil War turned out to be a West Pointers' war. In fifty-five of the sixty most

Many West Point graduates fought bravely and with distinction during the Civil War.

important battles of the war, West Pointers were in command on both sides.

During the first years of the war, General Robert E. Lee's Confederate forces won most of the major battles. But by 1865 the Union's larger forces, led by Ulysses S. Grant, had the Confederate troops reeling. Union troops were also helped by the fact that most of the country's industries and railroad lines were located in the North. The end of the war came in Virginia

ULYSSES S. GRANT

Ulysses S. Grant (left) graduated from West Point twenty-first out of thirty-nine students in the class of 1843. Years later, with the Civil War well under way, President Lincoln chose Grant to be the head of the Union army. By the time the war ended, Grant would be considered one of the greatest generals in history. He was the only general in the war to win the surrender of three enemy armies: at Fort Donelson in 1862, Vicksburg in 1863, and Appomattox in 1865.

Following the Civil War, Grant was elected president of the United States for two terms, from 1869 to 1877.

★ ★ ★ ★

on April 9, 1865. Lee and Grant met at the home of Wilmer McLean in Appomattox Court House, where Lee surrendered his army.

POST CIVIL WAR

After the Civil War the academy itself had challenges to meet. Advances in technology required changes in how wars were fought. Social changes required leaders within the academy to change the way they educated their cadets. During these changing times West Point had to continue to create effective soldiers while still staying true to its original goals.

During World War I, West Point graduates again distinguished themselves on the battlefield. After the war Douglas MacArthur, class of 1903, who had served as brigadier general during World War I, was named superintendent of West Point in 1919. MacArthur realized that West Point would have to make some changes in order to keep up with the physical demands of modern warfare. He upgraded the physical fitness program and encouraged participation in intramural athletics for all cadets. "Every cadet an athlete" became an important goal.

Douglas MacArthur was one of America's most famous generals. As superintendent of West Point, he made many changes in the school's curriculum, or course of study.

Leadership roles in World War II were filled by many U.S. Military Academy graduates. The impressive list was headed by future president Dwight Eisenhower and included Douglas MacArthur, Omar Bradley, and George Patton. The war and its aftermath saw breakthroughs in science and technology, an increased awareness of other cultures in the world, and an increase in the education level of soldiers. Once again the U.S. Military Academy made changes to meet the new needs.

In 1964, at the beginning of the buildup of U.S. forces in Vietnam, President Lyndon Johnson passed a law to increase the size of the Corps of Cadets from 2,529 to 4,417. It has since been reduced to about 4,000. A major

Taken around 1911, this photograph shows future president Dwight Eisenhower (third from left) as a member of the West Point Color Guard.

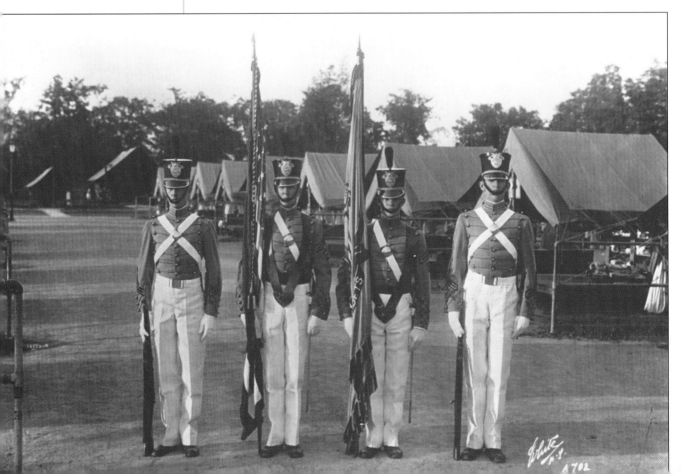

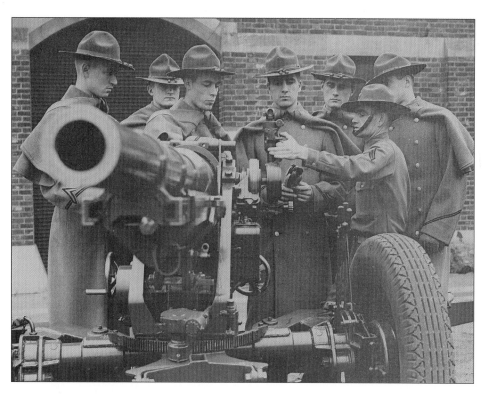

*   *   *   *

Before the start of World War II, cadets at West Point were taught how to use a 75 mm mobile gun.

expansion of facilities was begun in order to keep up with the growth of the Corps.

A DIVERSE STUDENT BODY

Since its earliest days, applicants to West Point have had to obtain a nomination, or recommendation, in order to be accepted into the U.S. Army as a cadet. The U.S. Military Academy is required by law to appoint cadets from every congressional district in the United States. Nominations may be made by the vice president of the U.S.; members of the U.S. Congress; congressional delegates from Washington, D.C., the Virgin Islands, and Guam; governors of Puerto Rico and American Samoa; and the Department of the Army

23

No matter where an applicant comes from or what his or her background is, he or she must meet tough acceptance standards.

(service-connected nomination). Each member of Congress may nominate up to ten candidates. Therefore, the student body is very diverse, or varied, and represents every region of the country.

AFRICAN AMERICANS AT THE U.S. MILITARY ACADEMY

In 1870 Congress directed West Point to accept African Americans as cadets. Henry Flipper was the first black cadet to graduate from West Point, in 1877. During his days as a cadet, he faced a great deal of racial **discrimination**, including the "silent treatment"—being excluded from all social conversations or activities—for all of his four years at the academy. Benjamin O. Davis faced the same treatment fifty-nine years later.

Finally, in 1948 President Harry S. Truman signed an executive order that outlawed racial discrimination at all government facilities, including West Point. Roscoe Robinson, Jr., class of 1951, became the first black four-star general in the U.S. Army when he was appointed in 1982. In 1987 Fred Gordon became the first African American commandant of the U.S. Military Academy at West Point. African-American graduates of the academy to date number 1,654.

Henry Flipper was the first African-American graduate of West Point. He later wrote a book about his experience called *The Colored Cadet at West Point.*

There are 103 African Americans in the class of 2004, making up about 9 percent of the class.

WOMEN AT WEST POINT

In 1975 President Gerald Ford signed a bill into law that allowed the admission of women into West Point. At the time, many cadets felt that women did not belong at West Point, as did many of the faculty members and senior officers. Initially, female cadets received tough treatment. Male cadets thought that women should be treated like men if they were to compete with them.

The first female cadets entered West Point in 1976. Four years later, Andrea Lee Hollen became the first woman to graduate from West Point. She was not the only woman in her class, but received that honor because she was the first to receive her diploma, based on class rank. Hollen went on to earn her masters degree at Oxford University, and retired from

Members of the Women's Army Corps (WAC) were the first women other than nurses to serve within the ranks of the U.S. Army.

Kristin Baker was the first female cadet to serve as First Captain, a cadet brigade commander.

the military in 1992 as a major. Kristin Baker, class of 1990, was the first female brigade commander. In the U.S. Corps of Cadets, this is the top-ranking leadership position. She is still in the military today and is stationed in Washington. The first female faculty member was appointed to West Point in 1977.

When cadets enter the academy they become active-duty members of the U.S. Army.

A WEST POINT EDUCATION

As members of the U.S. armed forces, cadets are paid a salary of $7,200, which helps them pay for uniforms, books, a personal computer, and other supplies. The U.S. government pays for the cadets' tuition, room and board, and medical and dental bills. When they graduate, cadets are commissioned, or appointed, as second lieutenants on active duty in the U.S. Army. They must serve for at least five years on active duty and three years in the reserves. This obligation satisfies the U.S. investment in each cadet's college education, currently valued at more than $250,000.

★ ★ ★ ★

Cadets are educated in three different areas: academics, military training, and athletics, with "a strong emphasis on moral-ethical development . . . woven into each." They must be able to manage their time in order to do well in all three. Many people wonder how West Point successfully teaches leadership, part of its self-stated mission. This is a question for which the academy does not claim to have an answer. Leadership is something that cannot be learned from a book or course alone. Perhaps the academy's success in teaching leadership skills comes partly from its careful selection of cadets and partly from the responsibilities the cadets are assigned throughout their four years there. It may also come from the academy's policy that every member of the West Point community act as a counselor or mentor. The academy's philosophy is that people learn best from being allowed to fail.

All cadets participate in hands-on military training that includes learning about basic soldier skills, military drills, and weaponry.

★ ★ ★ ★

MISSION STATEMENT

The academy's mission statement is "To educate, train, and inspire the Corps of Cadets so that each graduate is a commissioned leader of character committed to the values of Duty, Honor, Country; professional growth throughout a career as an officer in the United States Army; and a lifetime of selfless service to the nation." The U.S. Military Academy tries to accomplish this mission through a four-year process called the "West Point Experience."

Cadets receive a bachelor of science degree. They may choose from among nineteen majors. Some of the majors they may choose from are computer science, political science, history, literature, law, and mechanical engineering. West Point has graduated 58,000 cadets since its founding. Some became astronauts; others governors, members of Congress, businesspeople, and authors. Two West Point graduates were elected president—Ulysses S. Grant and Dwight Eisenhower—and six served as chairperson of the Joint Chiefs of Staff, the principal military adviser to the president.

Cadets are trained to use computers for a variety of military tasks.

A cadet slides a clipboard under the bedsheets to make certain that the fold in the sheet is up to military standards.

A DAY IN THE LIFE OF A CADET

Cadets wake up at 5 A.M., when they begin the job of putting a perfect crease in their pants and a perfect shine on their shoes. Their faces must be perfectly shaved. They

31

Students stand at attention before sitting down to breakfast.

brush their uniforms to remove all traces of lint. They clean their mirrors and sinks to remove all traces of toothpaste, and they inspect their closets and drawers to make sure all of their belongings are in order. Books have to be lined up in bookcases in size order. Even the socks in their drawers have to be folded in a certain way, and there is a daily inspection to ensure that cadets' barracks are in order.

At 6:55 A.M., the cadets march in formation to breakfast, which lasts for thirty-five minutes. Classes begin at 7:35 and last until 11:45. Lunch is served from 12:05 until 12:40. Cadets attend afternoon classes from 1:50 to 3:50. If they have no classes, they may use the time for study. Between 4:10 and 5:45, cadets participate in extracurricular activities, sports, and parades, and have free time. To allow cadets to make better use of their study time, they do not have to attend dinner in the mess hall. Instead, they can choose to have a "grab and go" meal. Study time runs from 8:30 to 11:30. Lights-out is at midnight.

After cadets finish their freshman year, they spend the summer at Camp Buckner, located 5 miles (8 km) outside the gates of West Point. At Camp Buckner, they practice riflery and marksmanship, night raids, armor, infantry **maneuvers**, field artillery, and receive other more advanced military training.

ARMY FOOTBALL

Athletics have long been an important part of academy life. Football, in particular, is a source of pride for West Pointers. At West Point, there is a feeling that what is being performed on the football field by its team serves a greater purpose. This feeling was strengthened by General Norman Schwarzkopf (class of 1956), commander of operations of Desert Storm, during a 1991 visit to the U.S. Military Academy. He told a group of cadets, "When your football team goes on the field, it does not go on the field with the name West Point. It does not go on the field with the name Cadets. When your football team goes on the field, you take the field with the name Army. And you are representing not only this student body and this institution, but you are representing everyone who proudly calls himself [or herself] a soldier."

Although the football teams at West Point and the U.S. Naval Academy have not been nationally ranked in many years, the Army-Navy game is still the highlight of the

Army-Navy football games attract scores of proud, loyal fans each year.

season for many college football fans. The first Army-Navy game was played on the Plain at West Point on November 29, 1890. Naval cadets had already been playing football at Annapolis for several years when Army's first and only game of the season was played.

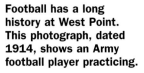
Football has a long history at West Point. This photograph, dated 1914, shows an Army football player practicing.

The first game was organized by Dennis Michie. Michie had played football while attending the Lawrenceville School. Over summer break, Michie received a friendly challenge from some U.S. Naval Academy midshipmen. Michie, the son of a West Point philosophy professor, asked the **administration** to support the creation of a team. He formed the first football team, coached it, and played halfback.

More than one thousand spectators attended the first Army-Navy game. Navy, being the more experienced team, won 24–0. This stimulated interest throughout the academy, and the next year, six games were scheduled for the team. The 1891 Army-Navy game was played at Annapolis, and this time Army won, 32–16. Michie helped coach two more teams before he graduated. On July 1, 1898, he was killed during the Spanish-American War. He was only twenty-eight years old when he became the first West Point football player to lose his life in battle. Michie Stadium is named in his honor.

THE MULE AND THE GOAT

In 1899, the cadets of West Point selected a mule as the Army mascot. At the time, the Navy mascot was a goat. Not knowing that mules are afraid of goats, the cadets were very embarrassed when their mascot ran away from the Navy's goat before the second game. The cadets kept their mule corralled with a goat for the entire year before the next game so he could get used to its smell, but at the third game, the mule ran away once again. This time the cadets got hold of two mules that weren't afraid of goats, and pregame festivities became a lot more fun.

Two cadets celebrate homecoming riding back to back on a mule, the school mascot.

Earl "Red" Blaik is shown here teaching plays to the Army football team in 1947.

A SECRET AND DANGEROUS MISSION

Traditionally, Army football players touch a plaque as they run into Michie Stadium at the beginning of each home game.

The plaque reads:

> *I want an officer for a secret and dangerous*
>
> *mission. I want a West Point football player.*
>
> —General George Marshall, Chief of Staff,
>
> U.S. Army, World War II

Army football entered its glory days under coach Earl "Red" Blaik, class of 1920. During his eighteen years as coach, Blaik coached two of the Army's three National Championship teams and three Heisman Trophy winners, Felix "Doc" Blanchard, Glenn Davis, and Pete Dawkins. Until 1984, Army vanished from the national rankings. That year, coach Jim Young led Army to its first bowl appearance and first bowl

＊ ＊ ＊ ＊

win, beating Michigan State in the Cherry Bowl. Today, Army's football team, the Black Knights, holds an impressive record and still attracts huge crowds.

DO YOU WANT TO BE A WEST POINT CADET?

To be accepted for admission to West Point, candidates are evaluated in several areas: academic performance, leadership skills, and physical aptitude. They must have good high school grades and high SAT or ACT scores, and have demonstrated leadership abilities in clubs and organizations. They must also pass a medical examination and be able to perform well on a **grueling** physical aptitude test.

Only applicants who have the right mental, physical, and moral qualities will graduate from West Point.

39

As cadets near the end of their four-year "West Point Experience," they are prepared to dedicate their lives to serving our nation.

West Point is looking for such leaders and scholars as class presidents, team captains, valedictorians, winners of academic awards, and high school athletes (the vast majority of West Point cadets played a varsity sport in high school). Candidates must be between seventeen and twenty-three years old on July 1 of the year they enter. They cannot be married or have legal responsibility to support a child.

In addition to these requirements, candidates must apply to the U.S. representative from their district, one of their state's senators, or the vice president of the United States to nominate them officially for admission.

It has been said that if you just want to become a general, there are schools better suited for your purpose, but if you want to become a great leader of people, the U.S. Military Academy at West Point is without equal. West Point—the academy, the **citadel**, the legend—is central to U.S. history.

> *If you leave here with the word Duty implanted in your mind; if you leave here with the word Honor carved in your soul; if you leave here with the word Country stamped on your heart, then you will be a twenty-first-century leader worthy—and I do mean worthy—of the great privilege and honor that you will have . . . of leading the magnificent young men and women who are the sons and daughters of America . . .*
>
> — General H. Norman Schwarzkopf, class of 1956

Glossary

administration—people who are in charge of managing an organization

artillerymen—armed soldiers

barracks—housing for soldiers

citadel—a military fort

discrimination—the singling out of one person or thing from another, usually in an unfair way

engineers—experts in the design and construction of something, usually engines, electrical equipment, or roads and bridges

grueling—very difficult and exhausting

maneuvers—military training exercises practicing the
    planned movement of troops

motto—a short sentence or phrase that serves as a
    guiding principle

promontory—a point of high land jutting out into an
    area of water

scouting—going ahead of a group to search out a
    particular area and gain information

sovereignty—freedom from outside control, independence

traitor—a person who betrays a trust

treason—working for the enemy; an act that is disloyal

Timeline: West Point

1777	1780	1802	1817	1861	1877	1919

George Washington, commander in chief of the Continental army, gives orders to fortify the spot at which the U.S. Military Academy at West Point stands today.

Benedict Arnold's plot to sell the plans to West Point to the British is uncovered.

President Thomas Jefferson signs an act establishing the U.S. Military Academy at West Point.

President James Monroe appoints Sylvanus Thayer superintendent of West Point.

The Civil War begins. Both Northern and Southern forces are commanded by West Point graduates.

Henry Flipper becomes the first African American cadet to graduate from West Point.

Douglas MacArthur is appointed superintendent of West Point.

1964

President Lyndon Johnson signs legislation increasing the size of the Corps of Cadets from 2,529 to 4,417.

1975

Gerald Ford signs a bill into law that allows the admission of women into West Point.

1980

Andrea Lee Hollen becomes the first woman to graduate from West Point.

2002

West Point celebrates its bicentennial.

To Find Out More

BOOKS

Gray, Valerie A. *The Court-Martial Trial of West Point Cadet Johnson Whittaker*. Berkeley Heights, NJ: Enslow Publishers, 2001.

Palmer, David Richard. *The River and the Rock: The History of the Fortress West Point, 1775–1783*. Brookfield, CT: Millbrook Press, 1996.

Sawyer, Susan. *The Army in Action*. Berkeley Heights, NJ: Enslow Publishers, 2001

Weintraub, Aileen. *Life Inside the Military Academy*. Danbury, CT: Children's Press, 2002.

ONLINE SITES

United States Military Academy at West Point
http://www.usma.edu

Military Training Picture Gallery
http://www.usma.edu/admissions/prosp_military_photos.asp

Index

Bold numbers indicate illustrations.

47

About the Author

Heidi Kimmel grew up in the Hudson Valley in a small town just north of West Point. She remembers walking the grounds, visiting the cemetery, and hiking up to Fort Putnam, which overlooks the academy, as a youngster. It made her feel that history was the story of real people, not just pages in old, dusty books. She could imagine George Washington, Edgar Allen Poe, George Custer, James Whistler, Ulysses S. Grant, and other famous Americans who attended West Point looking at the Hudson River from the very same place.

Kimmel graduated with a BA in English literature from Emerson College in Boston and went on to graduate studies in filmmaking. She worked as a high school English teacher before becoming a book editor and a technical writer. After living in California for many years, she moved back to the Hudson Valley and once again can visit West Point and other historic sites located nearby. She is married and has two sons, one of whom was lucky enough to attend summer baseball camp at West Point, stay in the main dorm, and eat his meals in the mess hall.